DARE TO PAIR

THE ULTIMATE GUIDE TO

CHOCOLATE AND WINE PAIRING

Another delicious book by Julie Nygard

Adapted from the author's book, *The Chocolate Therapist: A User's Guide to the Extraordinary Health Benefits of Chocolate*

Printed in the United States of America

ISBN-13: 978-1987464320
ISBN-10: 198746432X

For Britt and Blake. My life is
so much sweeter because you're in it.

CONTENTS

ACKNOWLEDGMENTS

Thank you to the thousands of people who have attended my classes and have been the guinea-pigs, testing wine after wine, chocolate after chocolate—it was a lot of work, but you hung in there. Thank you Ally and Rebekah, who helped bring the pairing process to a whole new level, and to the staff at The Chocolate Therapist. Thank you Mary Carol, chocolatier-extraordinaire. Thank you Dave, for always believing in me and for the endless hugs. And thank you Maryann, my peaceful graphic artist, for transforming the wild ideas in my mind into beautiful reality.

We've toasted abroad, we've toasted at home,
The chocolate enticing, never alone.

And along the journey, we discovered THE rule,
The precious secret of "Wine Pairing School"

If you ever discover a marginal pair,
Just keep drinking, my friend
And soon you won't care.

1 How It All Got Started

I know what you're thinking: chocolate and wine pairing is an interesting concept to say the least. When I first heard about it over a decade ago, my initial reaction was "why?" followed shortly after by "why not?" Fortunately, the job of learning about it came into my life out of sheer necessity. The work started shortly after the release of my book *The Chocolate Therapist*. A series of serendipitous events led to an opportunity to travel on cruise ships, giving lectures about chocolate. In the process of booking the first cruise, I was asked for the titles of *all* my lectures to confirm my reservation. This request surprised me because I'd only planned on lecturing about the health benefits of chocolate. But cruise ship policy calls for a series of lectures on the same topic, not the same topic five times. (I thought I'd share this fact with you in case you're thinking about presenting a topic on a cruise ship.)

I quickly came up with a series of lectures, keeping them simple and fun: "Chocolate and Wine Pairing," "Chocolate and Tea Pairing," "International Chocolates," "How to Throw a Chocolate Party," and, my original lecture, "The Extraordinary Health Benefits of Chocolate." I sent the list and secured my spot, a little later realizing that the only topic I knew anything about was the health benefits of chocolate. But I decided not to let a complete lack of knowing what I was doing stand in the way. Cruising to Bermuda and the Eastern Caribbean was on the line, so I'd have to figure it out.

I needed some practice fast. A bottle of wine and a box of chocolates seemed like a good place to start, and as I was polishing off my fourth pairing, it occurred to me that I might fare better doing the research with a group. If I did everything myself, it seemed unlikely that I'd fit into any of my clothes by the time the cruise date arrived. I also wanted to keep on track with the principle I was teaching in my lecture on the health benefits of chocolate: a person should eat between one and two ounces of good-quality dark chocolate a day at the most. This meant discovering a plan that didn't include a half pound of chocolate and a couple of glasses of wine a day (although the idea didn't seem half bad). I presented my idea for a chocolate- and wine-pairing class to Colorado Free University, a local continuing education facility. They loved the concept, and shortly thereafter I began teaching the classes, my experience limited to anything I could find in books (not much) and my own evolving list of pairings.

The first classes more than a decade ago were rather humorous—the perfect example of learning on the job. Although I'd researched every fact I could find about chocolate and wine pairing, putting it into a presentation didn't come naturally to me. I cut all the information into little pieces and meticulously reviewed every item with the class. It took hours to prepare for each class, and it was confusing for the students as they sifted through their folders, trying to find my notes on the chocolate or wine we were discussing. I also poured the wine into their glasses much too early, a strategy that in hindsight proved to be completely counterproductive. From the first sip, it was almost impossible to recapture anyone's attention. (I've since adopted a strict policy: education first, *then* drinking.) The classes were too long, and they contained too much information. And then there were the pairings, often frightful, as I used my early students as the unfortunate guinea pigs. (Note to self: Zinfandel and dark chocolate lemon is a definite NO.) Fortunately, we learned one of the cardinal rules of pairing early on: If you don't like a combination, just keep drinking! Eventually everything seems to pair perfectly.

I kept teaching and learning, adjusting and sharing, taking notes and revamping. I was committed to learning how to pair chocolate and wine. In the meantime having my class listed in Colorado Free University's catalog came with an unexpected benefit. The university sent the catalog out to thousands of people per quarter, and I soon found myself being asked to host corporate chocolate and wine events and private parties. People assumed that if I was teaching a class on the subject, I must know what I'm doing. I decided to bear the burden of my new "chocolate and wine pairing expert" title.

Somewhere during the early classes, I took my first cruise. The year was 2006. The cruise company asked me to prepare for about twenty to thirty guests, the average attendance for an enrichment lecturer. I considered this request and instead prepared for fifty guests. I was giving away free chocolate, after all, something that had probably never occurred on a cruise ship. It seemed likely that more than twenty people would show up. It was an eight-day cruise, and I had been asked to prepare four lectures. It seemed easy enough, but during the preparation I also had to discover the art of packing enough information for fifty people to attend four classes, while keeping the total weight of the materials under fifty pounds (to avoid the airline's heavy-bag fee). After repacking a mere seven times, I discovered that it *is* possible.

True to my estimate, I had excellent attendance for every class. On the day of the chocolate- and wine-pairing class, the room was filled with guests. Free wine and chocolate on a cruise ship? It was bound to be popular. With so many guests attending, the wine samples were so small they were barely recognizable, but people still loved the class. The cruise director was thrilled with the turnout. It helped, of course, that on my arrival I'd given her a signed book and a collection of chocolates to keep things moving smoothly. (Note: this is an excellent strategy for all speakers, even if you're not in the chocolate business.) Guests stayed long after the class was over and bought all of my books, even though that first edition of the book didn't include a chapter on chocolate and wine pairing. For the next five years, I took one to three cruises a year, traveling all over the world, teaching people about chocolate. I suppose someone had to do it.

Between cruises I spoke about chocolate's health benefits to any group that would listen. The first two years I spoke for free, surviving on after-event book sales and my fees from chocolate- and wine-pairing events. When demand exceeded my available time, I started to charge for the presentations, and things barely slowed down. (Note to self: I probably should have done that a little sooner.) Chocolate companies sponsored me in the beginning, but at some point I had my "aha" moment and decided to start my own brand. I developed a small line of chocolate bars to sell with the book while I was out speaking and hired a local company to manufacture the bars. Book sales doubled as soon as I had my own line, prompting another "I probably should have done that sooner" moment. It's true that we often only know exactly what to do in hindsight.

Everything was going great! I was selling thousands of books and chocolate bars, speaking regularly, and having lots of fun. The company making my bars was doing all the work. It seemed like a perfect arrangement to me. They must have gotten wise to the situation because right about this time, the owners decided to retire. My available choices: buy the shop or find a commercial kitchen. Having worked in retail when I was younger, I knew that buying a retail shop would be like having triplets—don't plan on going anywhere any time soon. It would be in direct contrast to my free-spirited entrepreneurial style.

Nonetheless, after thinking it through, I realized that I didn't want to manage production in someone else's commercial kitchen. After a few negotiations, I found myself the proud owner of a chocolate shop. Other than writing *The Chocolate Therapist*, my only experience in chocolate production was limited to a passion for making homemade chocolate-chip oatmeal cookies. I now owned a chocolate shop without any working knowledge about how to make chocolate. Time to put the entrepreneurial spirit to work.

I decided to add the story about purchasing the shop despite my lack of experience as proof that you don't have to know as much as you think to make something work. Whenever I give empowerment presentations to entrepreneurs, I encourage skipping the step that's stopping them and figuring it out later. Now I had to walk my own talk. Although I had extensive knowledge of nutrition when I wrote *The Chocolate Therapist*, I didn't know anything about chocolate, and things had been working out just fine with that. I asked myself, "How can this be any different?" Blind optimism is the perfect cliché simply because it works. I decided all I really needed was passion and purpose, and I had plenty of that.

The main chocolatier had stayed on after the purchase, which was quite helpful since I had no idea how to make chocolate. But just a month later, the person who had originally started the business twenty years earlier asked to come back and work at the shop, an unexpected stroke of good fortune because she was (and still is) an extraordinary chocolatier. Together we worked side by side for 10-12 hours a day to make it through the first Christmas. Welcome to the chocolate industry.

After working in the shop for a few months, one of the first things I decided to do was to change all the recipes. The chocolate shop I had purchased was more of a traditional shop--not overly committed to clean ingredients. For example, raspberry chocolates were filled with pink dyes and plenty of sugar. It was going to have to change, because my goal was to make chocolate that supported the pure eating concepts in my book *The Chocolate Therapist*. That meant creating products free from dyes, preservatives, or artificial ingredients of any kind. This is how I try to eat (to the extent that it's possible in today's world), and that's what *The Chocolate Therapist* is all about. It was important that everything we created in the shop reflected this message. The chocolatier and I went through the recipes, making changes and figuring out a way to create new products with all-natural ingredients.

People were a little surprised when we changed everything, especially considering I had no experience making chocolate. Many people told me it was a bad decision and that I'd lose customers (entrepreneur tip: when other people think it's a bad idea, you're usually on the right track). The other issue was that I couldn't be out there speaking about all-natural eating, then sending people to my shop to buy chocolate made with dyes and artificial flavors.

Up until that point, I'd been using a variety of brands for the chocolate- and wine-pairing events, but once we developed a clean ingredient line, I started using our new chocolates. I noticed right away how the pairings improved: pure chocolate and organic flavoring oils were far better than the mysterious ingredients of the other brands I'd been using. Our chocolates also contained considerably less sugar, which made them much better for pairing with wines and spirits.

I'd owned the shop for about eighteen months when business really started picking up. I hired an additional chocolatier who turned out to be a wine enthusiast. She and I started sampling wines and eating chocolate on a regular basis (it was tough). We stepped up the inventing process and tested out new chocolate concoctions with various wines. A year later, we enlisted the services of Groupon, a national online coupon and promotions company to help sell chocolate and wine pairing classes at the shop. We sold out every class for months. My wine-loving chocolatier learned how to teach the classes so that we could keep up with the demand. Looking back, I don't recall ever dreading going to work.

To get the information out to as many people as possible, this book, *Dare to Pair* became a necessary part of the process. Every event we hosted was always a great success, and each experience was unique. We discovered there was no terrible pairing because every palate is different: one person's miss is another person's perfect pairing (but skip the lemon dark chocolate with a red zinfandel to be sure). Fortunately, if you don't like the pairing, you still end up with a little chocolate and a little wine—just don't put them in your mouth at the same time.

It helps to have some basic strategies and ideas to start with when creating the optimal pairing experience. Over ten years of research is presented in *Dare to Pair*. Some of you will be tempted to zip right to the pairings; but without at least a small working knowledge of chocolate and wine pairing, there might be some confusion as to how to proceed. Personally, I think it's important to understand all the basics, so it's better to start at the beginning of the book and move on from there. Take a moment to skim the next sections if you're prone to leap ahead. You can always come back if you need a few more answers.

2 Chocolate and Wine Basics

News Breaks on Wine and Health

The news about red wine and heart health first came out in 1991 on *60 Minutes*. The phenomenon was called the French paradox, and the show focused on the fact that the French, who drink considerably more wine than Americans, have much lower levels of heart disease. The story ran twice that year, and Americans responded by increasing their purchases of red wine the following year by nearly 40 percent. *This* is how we embrace a health trend.

Similar information is now being released about the health benefits of chocolate. It's been more than a decade since the news broke, and we're finally seeing some "early adapter" healthcare professionals encouraging us to eat a little chocolate every day. As more research reveals the health benefits of dark chocolate, we're likely to see even more positive support.

Similarities between Chocolate and Wine

Chocolate and wine share many of the same qualities when it comes to pairing and tasting, the first being that both are fruits. We've known this about wine for centuries, but many people don't realize that chocolate is also made from the ground seeds of a fruit tree. The processing of chocolate and wine is also very similar. Cocoa processing involves harvesting the pods, splitting the pods and scooping out the beans, fermenting and roasting the beans, winnowing the nibs, and finally grinding the nibs into a thick chocolate soup called chocolate liquor—the basis of all things chocolate.

Wine starts with the harvest, followed by crushing the grapes, fermenting, blending (depending on the wine being produced), aging, and bottling the finished product. Both chocolate and wine are rich in antioxidants because both are made from the ground seeds of a fruit tree. Overall both processes are quite labor intensive, with many critical steps to get to the perfect finished product.

Both grapes and cacao grow in countries all over the world, but the distance from the equator varies between them. Cacao requires a hot, humid environment and grows in a band approximately ten degrees north and south of the equator. Grapes grow twenty to fifty-five degrees north and south of the equator, just outside the band of the cacao growing region. Because of this, grapes grow in an estimated seventy countries, whereas only thirty-three countries currently grow cacao.

Within various countries, cacao tree types change from region to region, and the taste of the beans also changes, just as grapes do. The trees pick up the nuances of the land and pass its flavors into the cacao beans. Similar characteristics are found in grape vines as well. There are hundreds flavor compounds in both wine and chocolate, making the possible combinations unlimited, so you better get started.

3 Proper Chocolate Consumption

Eating chocolate properly is an important step in appreciating a good pairing. In fact, people frequently come into our shop after having taken the chocolate and wine pairing class and mention how much they enjoyed the "proper chocolate consumption" part of the class. In general, people eat far too fast, so the intent of this section is to learn how to slow down. There's simply no way to discover the many flavor compounds that can be enjoyed in chocolate if it's in and out of your mouth in less than ten seconds. Food should arrive in your stomach in liquid form. How often does that actually happen?

This section requires your own personal flavor research. If you don't already have a piece of chocolate nearby, time to head toward the chocolate stash now (you know you have one). At the very least, sneak into the pantry for a handful of chocolate chips. Learning how to eat chocolate properly isn't that complicated and is well worth the effort.

There's a good chance you've never considered whether or not you eat chocolate properly. I'd been a devout consumer for decades, and the thought never entered my mind. I was amused to discover that there are actually published guidelines to assist with just such a task, as if we truly needed help. Once I read them, I discovered I'd been doing it wrong all along. Fortunately, having an imperfect technique didn't appear to affect my love for chocolate. Yet once I learned the correct procedure, it made all the difference because I started to enjoy chocolate more than I ever had. Slowing down actually made it taste better. Even if you have your own technique perfected, take a moment to review this section to make sure you're getting all the critical steps.

First of all, chocolate tastes best when eaten on an empty stomach. In the event that you find yourself with an empty stomach, this could be the perfect time for a chocolate tasting. I noticed the guidelines failed to mention what would happen if you *didn't* have an empty stomach. After some personal research, I concluded that regardless of the condition of your stomach, chocolate can be eaten without any negative side effects. (Although if you have ulcers, do not eat chocolate on an empty stomach because it has been reported to occasionally aggravate this condition.)

Now you're ready to begin the actual tasting. Pick up the chocolate and observe it as you would a work of fine art, taking time to examine its beauty and perfection. This step should last anywhere from five to twenty seconds. Since chocolate melts at 94°F, or slightly below body temperature, holding the chocolate starts the melting process, which helps release its aromas into the air. Gently wave the chocolate before your nose as you inhale the many tantalizing aromas. A large percentage of everything you taste comes from your sense of smell, so if you skip this step, you miss a considerable part of the experience.

Slowly place the chocolate on your tongue, allowing your lips to sense the gentle softness of the chocolate's texture. Let it sit in your mouth for a few seconds and begin melting on your tongue. Note the early flavors—is there anything unique, maybe a distinct flavor, or something unusual? As you start to chew, swirl the chocolate around your entire mouth. Note the texture—is it smooth, silky, gritty, flaky, chewy?

The idea is to allow the entire mouth to experience the chocolate. Some research claims that the tongue has four zones: salt, sour, bitter, and sweet. Yet more recent research suggests that the entire tongue tastes most flavors and that there are taste buds on the soft palate and upper epiglottis as well. Why take chances, though? Swirl it around for your own benefit, zones or no zones. Chocolate has hundreds of flavor compounds, and once you slow down and focus, you'll start to notice more of them.

Continue chewing as you swirl, but don't swallow just yet. Take a moment to press the chocolate onto the roof of your mouth with your tongue, savoring one last moment of melting and flavor euphoria. Relax, breathe deeply, and take in the lingering cacophony of sensations. Once you've completed this final step of delicious enjoyment, swallow at last. Note the flavors as they fade away: you may find something different that you didn't taste while it was in your mouth.

If you're sampling another type of chocolate, rinse your mouth thoroughly with water, light tea, or wine to prepare the palate for the next unique experience. Some connoisseurs insist on rinsing with water only because wine or tea can desensitize taste buds. Yet others recommend consuming chocolate with wine, which, of course, is what this book is all about. It seems like a personal preference to me—of course you should do exactly what you want. Fortunately, every choice wins because chocolate is involved in all cases.

The best way to learn about bean flavors is to sample single origin chocolates, meaning all of the cocoa beans that make up the bar have come from a single country. Since the beans pick up the nuances of the land where they're grown, different countries have very different flavor profiles. Once you've acquired the skills of an advanced connoisseur, you'll be able to discern a wide variety of bean flavors without even referring to the wrapper. Be prepared for an entertaining variety of subtle flavor sensations, such as spices, pepper, mango, pineapple, raspberry, cream, espresso, blueberry, lavender, almond, coffee, and even tobacco.

It's easier to identify flavors when you have them listed in front of you. To help train your palate, the "Blommer's Chocolate Wheel of Flavor," developed by Rose Potts of Blommer Chocolate Company, is included here. Once a piece of chocolate has thoroughly melted in your mouth, check the flavor wheel to help you uncover the mysteries. It seems obvious that you would know what you're tasting, but sometimes you won't remember a flavor until you see its name. With the wheel, you'll have dozens of choices in front of you.

The good news is that even if you've been eating chocolate incorrectly for years, no harm will come of it. My previous method involved directly placing the chocolate into my mouth (although not slowly, as advised), quickly chewing and then going straight for the next confection. The discovery of all the missing steps was a delightful surprise. Luckily, it's never too late to change. Once you've started making step-by-step adjustments, you may realize some of those steps are rather valuable. Pass the wine, please.

Blommer Chocolate Flavor/Aroma Wheel

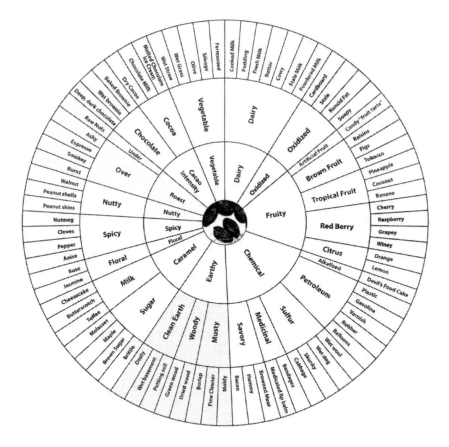

Use this chart to learn all the flavors of chocolate to become a discerning connoisseur.

The Chocolate Flavor/Aroma Wheel was developed by Rose Potts or Blommer's Chocolate Company. Permission granted to use this image by Blommer Chocolate Company. For your own flavor wheel, contact Blommer through their website at www.blommer.com.

4 Selecting the Proper Wine Glass

The next step is a brief review on how to enjoy wine from the correct glass. It's not imperative to have the precise glass, of course, but knowing the best choice gives you an option if you want to use it.

Anyone who has dined in the twenty-first century has undoubtedly noticed that various wines are served in different-shaped glasses. Entire classes are devoted to the topic, but to keep things simple, the following information is a condensed version of everything you need to know.

White-wine glass: Typically smaller than a red-wine glass for the purpose of concentrating the bouquet (or smell) in the glass. Make sure to breathe in the aromas before you sip to appreciate the wine from this glass. The wine glass is also slightly closed at the top to help maintain the temperature of the wine, which is primarily served chilled.

Red-wine glass: This larger, balloon-shaped glass helps oxidize the wine once it's out of the bottle, adding flavor and bouquet to the overall experience. Swirling the wine in the glass helps release the aromas and allows the flavors to expand.

Champagne glass: The long, fluted shape of this glass serves two purposes: it helps keep the Champagne cool and also releases the bubbles from a single point, preserving the Champagne just a bit longer.

Port glass: The primary reason for the smaller size of this glass is to allow you to enjoy a full glass while drinking a smaller amount of port. The unusual expense of port makes the smaller glass a good concept for dining establishments but not such a good value for the consumer. On a positive note, considering the higher alcohol content of port along with the likelihood that you'll be drinking it closer to the end of the evening, the smaller glass also serves as protection against the possibility of overindulging.

How to Taste Wine

Just like chocolate, there are published guidelines on how to taste wine properly. If you're like most people, you've been drinking wine without much consideration for years. But it's time to step up your game, get focused and truly learn how to enjoy a glass of wine.

Ideally, your wine should be poured into the proper glass for maximum flavor and aroma. In case you skipped that section, it's right before this one and takes less than two minutes to read.

Red wine is normally served at room temperature and should be opened before you serve it to help aerate the wine, although not much happens in that regard unless it's poured into a decanter. To really release the aromas and aerate red wine, pour it into a larger container and let it sit for 20-45 minutes. White wine, on the other hand, is normally served chilled, although depending on the type can also be served at room temperature.

Next pour the wine into the glass and observe the color. Some people prefer to hold a white cloth or napkin to the back of the glass to get a true assessment of color. The depth of the color can indicate the intensity of the flavor.

Swirl the wine in the glass to help release its aroma and nuances. While it runs back down the side of the glass, note the viscosity. If you see the wine running down the glass, it's said to have "legs." Take a long sniff or two to stimulate your olfactory glands and help wake up your taste buds. Smell is accountable for a major percent of everything you taste, so it's in your best interest to take time for this step.

Next take a small sip of the wine, but don't swallow immediately. Keep it in your mouth and swirl it around your tongue, looking for flavor notes such as fruit, oak, earth, mineral, sweet, sour, bitter, and salty. Observe the texture—is it smooth, light, full, or delicate?

Try taking a breath though your nose with the wine still in your mouth. Think carefully about this procedure, as taking a breath while swallowing could cause some problems. The key, of course, is not to swallow exactly at the same time you're breathing.

The last step, finally, is to swallow. But your job isn't finished! How long does the flavor last? What are the lingering nuances? Is it sweet, acidic, robust, tannic, or strong in alcohol? There are so many things to consider. You may have to take another sip or two to get it right.

To help with flavor identification, see the "Wine Aroma Wheel" by Ann Noble on the next page. Having the flavors at your fingertips can help you determine a wine's exact essences and aromas. The strategy here is the same as the "Blommer Chocolate Wheel of Flavor." Once you have the wine in your mouth, look at the different flavors on the wheel to help you discern what you are tasting.

The Wine Aroma Wheel

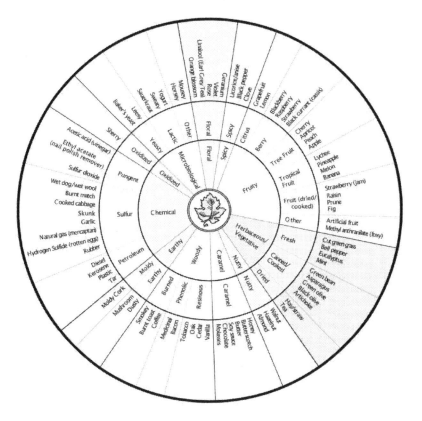

This is an excellent reference for discovering and learning
the flavors in wines.

Putting It All Together

People always ask me what they should put in their mouth first when pairing—the wine or the chocolate? Personally, I prefer to put the chocolate in my mouth first, taking special care to follow the proper chocolate consumption instructions as noted earlier. This gives the chocolate a chance to melt before you add the wine. If the wine is cool and you drink it before eating the chocolate, it can lower the temperature of your mouth and make it harder to taste all the flavors in the chocolate.

As you're assessing the chocolate, pour about a third of a glass of wine. Swirl the wine in the glass and take short sniffs, as reviewed in "How to Taste Wine." I prefer to take a small sip and swish the wine around with the chocolate so the two mingle together. Note how the flavors of the chocolate have changed. Some of the flavors will be accentuated by the wine; others will be covered up. Sometimes the wine is too strong for the chocolate, or the chocolate may be too strong for the wine. In fact, if you find the pairing is "biting" or "puckering" in your mouth, try them separately—first the wine, then chocolate or vice versa. You're looking for balance. The perfect pairing accentuates both the wine and the chocolate.

After you've paired the wine and chocolate in this order, you may want to reverse the process and drink the wine first, followed by eating the chocolate. Remember to go slowly: smell the wine, take a small sip, and note the flavors, then add the chocolate and note how the flavors of both the chocolate and the wine change. If you rush, this takes away from the process, and you'll miss quite a few of the flavors. Remember, there are hundreds of flavors between the chocolate and the wine, and there's no right or wrong. In fact, as mentioned previously, we jokingly say "if you find a pairing you don't like, just keep drinking!"

Before you switch to the next pairing, cleanse your palate with bland crackers or water. A salt-free table cracker works well because the goal of a palate cleanser is to neutralize the palate. I prefer to stay away from salt because it changes the palate considerably, and it changes the flavor of chocolate as well. It's also best to drink room temperature water to keep your mouth warm.

5 Red Wine and Chocolate Pairings

For pairing purposes note that wines are generally classified into three different body types: light, medium, and full. A light-bodied wine is in and out of your mouth quickly, and you taste it only while it's in your mouth. It's also typically lighter in color, and you can see through it. Lighter reds generally have higher acidity levels and are best drunk when relatively young. Open a bottle of light-bodied red wine, and you'll want to finish the bottle immediately. Examples of lighter reds include pinot noir, gamay, Beaujolais, and an occasional merlot.

A medium-bodied wine lingers awhile once you've swallowed it, allowing you to assess the taste and aftertaste longer than the lighter wines. It's generally a moderate shade of red or burgundy. It contains more tannins than the lighter reds, although you'll still want to enjoy this wine right after opening the bottle. Leave it around longer than four days, and much of the flavor will be gone. To stretch out its life, put it in the refrigerator to help keep it from oxidizing. Examples of medium-bodied wines include

Grenache, Carmenere, Carignan and Cabernet Franc, although these wines can be full-bodied as well.

Full-bodied wine flavors last long after the wine has been swallowed and offer changing taste sensations on the finish. The color is deep and rich—not something that can easily be gazed through. The fullest wines also have the highest level of tannins. Full-bodied wines last a little longer as well. After two days, you may discover flavors you didn't notice on opening. Examples of full-bodied wines include cabernet sauvignon, Petite Verdot, and Shiraz.

The details provided for each wine in the pairing section that follows are general, and you won't taste every flavor listed for each wine. Flavors depend on many elements, such as growing regions, production techniques, the average temperature during the growing season, and more. The following are flavors you *may* find in each wine, although flavors vary considerably depending on the country, region and style of winemaking. They're included here because having a list will help you discern flavors you might not otherwise be able to identify. You can also refer to popular wine apps such as Vivino, Wine Searcher and Delectable. Each app offers slightly different features, so investigate and download the one that serves your personal wine style.

All recipes identified by an asterisk (*) can be found in the back of this book.

AMARONE

Grapes used to make: Corvina, Rondinella, Sangiovese, Molinara

Regions grown in: Italy/Veneto

Body: Full bodied, soft tannins, higher alcohol, often dry, long flavor

Flavors: Dried fruit, ripe wild berries, candied fruit, chocolate, charcoal, cinnamon, baked cherries, smoke, truffle, port, earth

Notes: Whatever you're serving, make sure it's powerful enough to withstand the strength of this powerful (and expensive) Italian wine. It's a great wine for foods with bold tastes; Try a dark chocolate mole' sauce over chicken.

Chocolate Pairings

- Safe: Dark chocolate cherry truffle
- Adventurous: Dark chocolate pecan brownies covered with Raspberry/Pomegranate Puree*

BARBARESCO

Grapes used to make: Nebbiolo

Regions grown in: Italy/Piedmont, California

Body: Medium to full bodied, bold, spicy, tannic, elegant, good balance, long on palate; a powerful wine that holds up well with bold flavors

Flavors: Earth, fig, nut, leather, tar, mushroom, vanilla, cinnamon, plum, raspberry, black cherry, violet, rose, sweet red fruit, licorice, menthol, mineral, spice

Notes: Two of the hallmark flavors of Barbaresco are cherry and roses, so try something totally unexpected with a rose truffle. One of my favorite eclectic truffle companies is Robin Chocolates. (www.RobinChocolates.com). Robin was named by Dessert Professional as one of the Top Ten Chocolatiers in North America in 2013, so prepare for the taste-tantalizing brilliance of her award-winning truffles. Barbaresco's rich flavors make it an adventurous experience with chocolate.

Chocolate Pairings

- Safe: Single-origin dark chocolate from Ecuador, known for its deep, earthy flavor
- Adventurous: Raspberry Truffle Brownies*

♈ BARBERA ♈

Grapes used to make: Nebbiolo

Regions grown in: Italy/Piedmont, California

Body: Medium bodied, smooth, low tannins with high acidity

Flavors: Blackberries, plum, black pepper, cinnamon, vanilla, strawberry, spice, cherry, raspberry, earth, cranberry, pomegranate

Notes: This wine is particularly suited to Mediterranean foods, making it ideal for pairing with fruits from the same region, such as red currants, cranberries, and gooseberries.

Chocolate Pairings

- 🍫 **Safe: Milk and dark chocolate together, melted and lightly swirled**
- 🍫 **Adventurous: Double Dark Chocolate Brownies* topped with a sprinkle of chili pepper**

♈ BAROLO ♈

Grapes used to make: Nebbiolo

Regions grown in: Italy/Piedmont, California

Body: Medium to full bodied, rich, heavy, robust, high in acidity, tannin and alcohol

Flavors: Black cherry, leather, earth, mushroom, chocolate, floral, rose, herbs, berries, coconut, vanilla, raspberry, spice, oregano, tobacco, anise, violet

Notes: Make sure to open your wine early and let it breathe for at least an hour to make sure it aerates properly. This allows the flavors to open up, making it easier to pair the wine with chocolate.

Chocolate Pairings

- Safe: **Dark chocolate tart**
- Adventurous: **Berry cobbler lightly drizzled with melted 75% dark single-origin Madagascar chocolate**

BEAUJOLAIS

Grapes used to make: Gamay

Regions grown in: France/Burgundy region of Beaujolais, Switzerland, Oregon, New Zealand

Body: Light body, low tannins

Flavors: Cranberry, cherries, raspberry, strawberries, black currants, cedar, earth, leather, floral

Beaujolais: Made from 100 percent gamay grapes, generally light and fruity

Beaujolais Nouveau: The lightest, fruitiest, and youngest of the Beaujolais family. The time from harvest to retail is often less than two months. Once you open the bottle, consume it within hours or there will hardly be anything left to taste.

Beaujolais Villages: A step up from Nouveau, Beaujolais Villages wines are produced in regions known to produce higher-quality grapes.

Beaujolais Cru: The best Beaujolais money can buy. Look for the word *cru* on the label.

Notes: When considering chocolate, go for the lighter dark chocolate, such as 45 to 55 percent dark with fruity and/or nutty nuances. Very dark chocolate will bury the wine, and you'll end up with bitterness. Also note that citrus and cream flavors can clash with Beaujolais.

Chocolate Pairings

- Safe: 55 percent dark chocolate with fresh or dried raspberries
- Adventurous: Devils' food cake topped with fresh strawberries

BORDEAUX

Grapes used to make: Generally a combination of different grapes, including cabernet sauvignon, merlot, cabernet franc, Malbec, and Petit Verdot.

Regions grown in: France/Bordeaux, Italy

Body: Medium to full bodied, soft to moderate tannins, smooth

Flavors: Oak, blackberry, Indian spices, licorice, green olive, dark olive, plum, mineral, flowers, jam, cherry, strawberry, smoke, earth, cassis, black currant, dried herbs, toast, herb, vanilla, cedar, roasted coffee, mocha, cola

<u>Notes:</u> Bordeaux is any wine produced in the Bordeaux region of France, so narrowing the field of flavors and grapes is almost impossible. Read the labels to determine the flavors of your Bordeaux, and then select the chocolate accordingly.

Chocolate Pairings

- Safe: Chocolate mocha-flavored mousse
- Adventurous: Cherry pie drizzled with milk or dark chocolate

BRUNELLO

Grapes used to make: Brunello, Sangiovese

Regions grown in: Italy/Tuscany

Body: Full bodied, generally longer on finish, strength in tannins

Flavors: Blackberry, vanilla, red pepper, currant, toasted oak, cherry, berry, anise, menthol, leather, tobacco, espresso, raspberry, blueberry, plums

Notes: Brunello is the signature wine of Italy's Montalcino region, considered by some to be one of Italy's best wines. Unexpected bold flavors and aromas keep the chocolate pairing options wide open for negotiation, so if you don't see something that piques your palate here, investigate a collection of your own concoctions.

Chocolate Pairings

- **Safe: Raspberry Dark Chocolate Truffles***
- **Adventurous: Dark chocolate with cinnamon and ginger**

BURGUNDY

Grapes used to make: Pinot noir, less expensive wines may also include gamay

Regions grown in: France/Burgundy

Body: Medium to full bodied; full, ripe tannins; long finish

Flavors: Raspberry, plum, spice, flowers, blackberry, cherry, leather, earth, pomegranate, vanilla, chocolate, apple, pineapple, banana, mayflower, hazelnut

Notes: The Burgundy region in France produces both red and white wines. A true red Burgundy is made only from the pinot noir grape, although less expensive versions may include gamay grapes as well. Blends are considered second class to the great Burgundies of the region.

Adventurous Chocolate Pairings

- **Safe: Molten Chocolate Lava Cake**
- **Adventurous: Pomegranate and Cinnamon Double Dark Chocolate Brownies***

🍷 CABERNET FRANC 🍷

Grapes used to make: Cabernet franc, cabernet sauvignon, merlot

Regions grown in: France/Bordeaux and Loire Valley, California/Napa Valley, Washington State, Chile, South Africa, Spain

Body: Medium to full bodied, gentle tannins, high acidity

Flavors: Raspberries, strawberry, cinnamon, plum, pepper, dried cherry, cedar, spice, green peppers, cocoa powder, savory, flowers, earth, tarragon

Notes: For a most tasteful wine, decant for 30 minutes to settle Cab Franc's natural spiciness. This versatile wine often contains chocolate notes on the finish, making it a natural for pairing.

Chocolate Pairings

 Safe: Dark chocolate with cherries, cranberries and blueberries (available at www.TheChocolateTherapist.com)

🍫 **Adventurous: Mint Double Dark Chocolate Mousse***

🍷 CABERNET SAUVIGNON 🍷

Grapes used to make: Cabernet sauvignon (at least 75 percent), merlot, Shiraz

Regions grown in: France/Bordeaux, California (mostly dry cabs), Australia (always dry), Chile, Argentina, Italy, Spain, Washington State

Body: Full bodied, robust, hearty, big tannins, acidic, deeply colored, concentrated flavors, dense, structured

Flavors: Dark chocolate, black currant, tobacco, blackberry, plum, cherry, mint, green pepper, bitter, woody, vanilla, earth, Havana leaf, espresso, licorice, blueberry, violet, eucalyptus, spice, truffles, leather, toasty oak

Notes: For centuries, cabernet sauvignon reigned as the world's most planted premium grape, an arguable statement as some sources claim it's the Grenache grape. Drop back to 2005 and most sites report merlot as number one. Regardless of its status, the cabernet grape's thick skins make for a bold, tannic, and widely flavorful wine.

Chocolate Pairings

- 🍫 **Safe: Dark chocolate infused with mint oil (available at www.TheChocolateTherapist.com)**
- 🍫 **Adventurous: Flourless chocolate torte with a raspberry pomegranate puree***

♉ CHIANTI ♉

Grapes used to make: Sangiovese (80%), cabernet sauvignon, merlot, Syrah

Regions grown in: Italy/Tuscany, California/Napa Valley

Body: Light to medium bodied, bright acidity, higher in tannins, tannic finish

Flavors: Cherry, tobacco, coffee, apple, leather, herb, chocolate, intense dark fruit, vanilla, red plum, cedar, violet, raspberry

Notes: This Italian wine pairs perfectly with Italian entrées like seasoned meats, pizza, sausage, and pasta. It's a bit challenging to pair with dessert, but since you're already most likely enjoying an Italian entrée, why not venture out with an Italian-themed dessert like chocolate tiramisu, a double chocolate hazelnut biscotti, or even a chocolate tortoni?

Chocolate Pairings

- 🍫 **Safe: Milk Chocolate Orange Meltaway (available at www.TheChocolateTherapist.com)**
- 🍫 **Adventurous: Chocolate tiramisu**

🍷 DOLCETTO 🍷

Grapes used to make: Dolcetto

Regions grown in: Italy/Piedmont, Australia, California (where the grapes are called douce noire), New Zealand, Canada

Body: Light to medium bodied, low acid

Flavors: Black cherry, licorice, almond, prune, fruit, jam

Notes: *Dolcetto* translates to "little sweet one," but don't look for a little, sweet wine here. While the name implies "wine cuteness," the soft and fruity grape still delivers a nice tannic snap. In years past it was a lighter wine, but more recently it's being made in a bolder style, making it better to pair with chocolate.

Chocolate Pairings

- **Safe: Chocolate-covered dried Bing cherries**
- **Adventurous: Dark Chocolate Cake with Chocolate Apricot Glaze* topped with sliced almonds**

🍷 GRENACHE 🍷

Grapes used to make: Grenache

Regions grown in: France, Spain, Italy, California, Australia

Body: Medium

Flavors: Raisin, currant, spice, blackberry, raspberry, cherry, blueberry, cinnamon, strawberry, vanilla

Notes: Grenache is one of the most widely planted grapes in the world, and many consider it as important as cabernet sauvignon. Because it can bring fruitiness and body without added tannins, it can fabulous when paired with chocolate.

Chocolate Pairings

- 🍫 Conservative: Dried orange peel dipped in dark chocolate
- 🍫 Adventurous: Dark chocolate and chili pepper, either as a truffle or melt dark chocolate and sprinkle with a little spicy chili pepper

MALBEC

Grapes used to make: Malbec, cabernet sauvignon, occasionally Tannat

Regions grown in: Argentina, France/Bordeaux

Body: Full, refreshing acidity, sweet tannins

Flavors: Black fruits, blackberry, plum, leather, vanilla, spice, raspberry, cherry, violet, black pepper, chocolate, tobacco, smoke, pomegranate

Notes: Malbec originated in the Cahors region of France, but now more than 75% of it is grown in the Mendoza region of Argentina. Although the both regions grow the same grape, the wines are quite different. French Malbec has more structure with savory and blackberry notes, whereas wines from Argentina tend to be fruit-forward, smooth and plummy

Chocolate Pairings

- 🍫 Safe: Coffee Ganache Truffles*
- 🍫 Adventurous: Chocolate covered ginger

MERITAGE

Grapes used to make: Cabernet sauvignon, merlot, cabernet franc, Petit Verdot, Malbec, Carmenere, Gros Verdot. Meritage wines have a required 75% minimum blend of Bordeaux grape varietals.

Regions grown in: California/Napa Valley, Washington State, Chile

Body: Medium to full bodied with a long finish, can have smooth and soft tannins

Flavors: Dark berries, cherry, spice, coffee, dark cocoa, black olive, flowers, plum, toasty oak, berry cobbler, clove, vanilla, blackberry

Notes: The word *meritage* comes from a combination of the words *merit* and *heritage*, used to describe wines of merit with superior heritage. The wine is made in a "Bordeaux style," although not on French soil. For the term to be used on the label, the release must be less than twenty-five thousand bottles and cannot be sold as a "bargain" wine.

Chocolate Pairings

- **Safe: Milk or dark chocolate lightly sprinkled with fresh ground espresso**
- **Adventurous: Dark chocolate fondue with an array of fresh berries for dipping**

MERLOT

Grapes used to make: Merlot, cabernet sauvignon

Regions grown in: France/Bordeaux, Italy, Australia, California/Napa Valley, Chile, Argentina, South Africa, New Zealand, Washington State, Long Island

Body: Medium bodied, soft tannins, supple texture, smooth, rich, easygoing flavor

Flavors: Black cherry, blackberry, raspberry, cassis, plum, violet, raisin, clove, coffee, dark chocolate, wild blueberry, vanilla

Notes: A broadly versatile wine, merlot spans the food charts in pairing. When venturing in chocolate, think black cherry, amaretto, raspberry and orange and you'll have a nice start.

Chocolate Pairings

 Safe: Chocolate poppy seed cake drizzled with dark chocolate

 Adventurous: Dark chocolate peanut butter cup

MOURVEDRE

Grapes used to make: Mourvedre, often blended with Grenache, Syrah, or other Rhone region grapes to improve its color and structure

Regions grown in: Italy, Australia/Barossa Valley, California/Napa Valley, Washington State, Spain, France

Body: Full-bodied, high tannins, moderate acidity

Flavors: Blueberry, blackberry, plum, savory meats, smoke, raspberry, cherry, apricot, chocolate, coffee, leather, black pepper

Notes: The high tannic character of this wine make it especially good with rich dishes or sauces, which tend to balance it out. Mourvedre's unique blend of earthy, gamey, and light red fruit flavors means you don't have to stop drinking just because dinner has ended—enjoy it with dessert too!

Chocolate Pairings

 Safe: Chocolate chip oatmeal cookies* dipped in dark chocolate

 Adventurous: Chocolate Cream Pie

NEBBIOLO

Grapes used to make: Nebbiolo

Regions grown in: Italy/Piedmont, California/Napa Valley, Washington State, Argentina, Australia

Body: Medium to full bodied, high tannins for a long, fresh finish, although it can be quite tannic when it's younger

Flavors: Rose, ripe fruit, spices, licorice, blackberry, oak, raspberry, cherry, glycerin, coffee, chocolate, smoke, tobacco, plum, tar, herbs, prune

Notes: This late-harvest grape (October) forms the base some of Italy's most well-known wines, including Barolo and Barbaresco. It's typically a highly acidic grape, and wines made from the Nebbiolo pair best with the darker chocolates and intensely flavored infusions and inclusions.

Chocolate Pairings

- **Safe: Melted dark chocolate with dried cherries and cinnamon**
- **Adventurous: Apple/Blackberry pie* with dark vanilla chocolate drizzle***

♟ PETITE SIRAH ♟

Grapes used to make: Petite Sirah, often blended with zinfandel to give density and structure. The grape is also called Durif.

Regions grown in: California/Napa Valley, Australia, France, Israel

Body: Full bodied, full tannins, smooth, lasting finish, high acidity, deeply colored

Flavors: Blueberry, plum, blackberry, black pepper, ink, ripe fruits, toasty oak, pomegranate, vanilla, dark chocolate, spice, anise, mocha, smoke

Notes: Like the bold Nebbiolo, this energetic wine is best paired with hearty chocolates and rich, flavorful infusions and inclusions. Its high acidity can easily bury a milder chocolate, so think big—70% dark and higher.

Chocolate Pairings

- **Safe: Berry and chocolate tart**
- **Adventurous: Chili Pepper Patties (available at www.TheChocolateTherapist.com)**

PINOT NOIR

Grapes used to make Pinot noir

Regions grown in: France/Beaujolais and Burgundy, California, Oregon/Willamette Valley, Australia, South Africa, Germany, Switzerland, New Zealand, Italy

Body: Light to medium bodied, mild to moderate tannin, prominent acidity

Flavors: Cherry, raspberry, earth, leather, vanilla, jam, plum, licorice, cedar, mushrooms, strawberry, chocolate, mixed berries, smoke, violet, Asian spices, oak

Notes: A good pinot noir works with practically everything, from potato chips to roasted chicken and mushroom risotto. But take note when adding chocolate: give the wine a chance by looking for a lighter chocolate, such as dark milk or light dark, 45-55% to make sure you don't over power the wine.

Chocolate Pairings

- 🍫 **Safe: Brie and chocolate covered strawberries**
- 🍫 **Adventurous: Flourless chocolate torte drizzled with raspberry purée and sprinkled with finely chopped almonds**

PORT, RUBY

Grapes used to make: Over one hundred grapes can be used in port, but the primary five are Tinta Barroca, Tinta Cao, Tempranillo, Touriga Francesa, and Touriga Nacional

Regions grown in: Portugal/Douro, Canada, Australia, India, Argentina, South Africa, United States

Body: Full bodied, fortified (clear brandy is added to port), beautiful deep red colors

Flavors: Dark fruit, red berries, strawberry, raspberry, cherry, raisins, dates

Notes: One way to remember which port pairs best with which chocolate is to think about color. Ruby ports generally pair well with chocolate with ruby or red-colored fruits like cherries, raspberries, cranberries, strawberries, and pomegranate. Tawny port (see the next category) works well with tan-colored inclusions such as nuts, spices, caramel, and toffee.

Chocolate Pairings

- **Safe: Milk chocolate drizzled over a fresh fruit tart**
- **Adventurous: Dark chocolate infused with organic black cherry oil (available at www.TheChocolateTherapist.com)**

🍷 PORT, TAWNY 🍷

Grapes used to make: Over one hundred grapes can be used in port, but the primary five are Tinta Barroca, Tinta Cao, Tempranillo, Touriga Francesa, and Touriga Nacional.

Regions grown in: Portugal/Douro, Canada, Australia, India, Argentina, South Africa, United States

Body: Full bodied, fortified (clear brandy has been added)

Flavors: Nuts, pepper, fruit, caramel, toffee, black currant, maple syrup, apricot, orange, date, smoke, spice, cream, apricot

Notes: Tawny port is more delicate and flavorful than ruby port. Just as with ruby port, the easiest way to remember what pairs well with it is to think about color. Tawny ports are tan in color, so they work well with chocolates that have tan-colored inclusions like spices, caramel, toffee, and nuts. Cinnamon is particularly good with tawny port, so try creating a few of your own cinnamon-infused adventures.

Chocolate Pairings

- **Safe: Milk-chocolate-covered cinnamon pecans (www.TheChocolateTherapist.com)**
- **Adventurous: Pecan pie drizzled with dark chocolate**

♈ RIOJA ♈

Grapes used to make: Tempranillo, Garnacha Tinta, Mazuelo, Graciano. True Riojas are composed of primarily Tempranillo (60 percent), and Garnacha (20 percent), with the other varietals making up the difference.

Regions grown in: Northern Spain

Body: Medium to full bodied, elegant, soft, high alcohol, full and ripe tannins

Flavors: Fruits, strawberry, oak, vanilla, plum, dark chocolate, cherry, berry, nut, earth, graphite, espresso roast, black currant

Notes: The popular Rioja Gran Reserva wine spends at least two years in an oak barrel and three years in the bottle. Oak and vanilla are the featured flavors, making a vanilla-infused chocolate dessert the perfect partner in pairing.

Chocolate Pairings

- 🍫 **Safe: Dark chocolate mocha mousse**
- 🍫 **Adventurous: Black Forest cherry cake with Chocolate Whipped Cream**

♈ SANGIOVESE ♈

Grapes used to make: Sangiovese, (when cabernet sauvignon, merlot, and Syrah are added, these varietals make up the Super Tuscan wines)

Regions grown in: Italy/Tuscany, California, Argentina, Romania, France, Australia

Body: Light to medium bodied, moderate to high acidity, high tannin

Flavors: Earth, herbal, fig, tart cherry, strawberry, blueberry, floral, plum, violet, orange, clove, cinnamon, thyme

Notes: As Professional Friends of Wine puts it on its site, "Sangiovese is to Chianti as Cabernet Sauvignon is to Bordeaux." These grapes form the base of the respective wines, although they are enjoyable on their own as well. When pairing with chocolate, focus on dark chocolates with a lower percentage of cocoa so you don't overpower the wine.

Chocolate Pairings

- 🍫 **Safe: Dark chocolate cake with orange reduction sauce**
- 🍫 **Adventurous: Milk chocolate infused cinnamon, ginger, and clove (available at www.TheChocolateTherapist.com, Wine Pairing Chocolates / Mulling Spice)**

SHIRAZ/SYRAH

Grapes used to make: Shiraz, Viognier, Grenache, Mourvedre, cabernet sauvignon. Shiraz is almost always blended with other grapes.

Regions grown in: Australia, California, South Africa, France/Rhone Valley. The name Shiraz is primarily used for wines from Australia, South Africa, Argentina, Chile, and Canada, while France and the United States use Syrah. It's the same grape masquerading under separate names.

Body: Full bodied, generally powerful, robust, long lived, tannic

Flavors: Blackberry, boysenberry, black pepper, tar, black fruits, plum, raspberry, licorice, dark chocolate, black currants, caramel, toast, blueberry, vanilla, earth, wood, herb, cinnamon

Notes: A quick preview of the many flavors in Shiraz and it's hard to imagine a chocolate that *doesn't* pair with it. A typically spicy grape, it works nicely with spice-infused chocolates and especially well with eclectic truffles.

Chocolate Pairings

- 🍫 **Save: Fruit and nut dark chocolate fondue**
- 🍫 **Adventurous: Dark chocolate sprinkled with New Mexican chili pepper**

🍷 TEMPRANILLO 🍷

Grapes used to make: Tempranillo, also one of the most used grapes for Port and Rioja

Regions grown in: Spain, Argentina, South Africa, California/Napa Valley, Australia, Canada

Body: Medium to full bodied, soft, long on finish, low sugar, higher acidity when younger

Flavors: Cherry, dried fig, raspberry, truffles, smoke, spices, tobacco, leather, herb, plum, strawberry, vanilla, cedar

Notes: Like many reds, chocolate and berries are usually a good bet when pairing. Treat it like other full-bodied reds by edging your chocolate toward the darker side.

Chocolate Pairings

- 🍫 **Safe: Dark chocolate mint brownies (add one-half teaspoon of mint to your favorite recipe)**
- 🍫 **Adventurous: Hazelnut biscotti dipped in milk or dark chocolate**

🍷 VALPOLICELLA 🍷

Grapes used to make: Corvina Veronese, Rondinella, Molinara

Regions grown in: Italy/Veneto and Valpolicella

Body: Light to medium body, full flavor, long finish

Flavors: Cherry, raspberry, strawberry, jam, milk chocolate, licorice, smoke, wood, spice, oak, black fruit

Notes: Valpolicella is produced two ways—traditional and modern. Each style has its own characteristics, but the modern method (new oak aging)

tends to give it more chocolate-friendly pairings because it ads molasses, cherry and chocolate flavors

Chocolate Pairings

- 🍫 **Safe: Dark or milk chocolate cinnamon truffles***
- 🍫 **Adventurous: Double mocha chocolate brownies* with Chocolate Whipped Cream***

🍷 ZINFANDEL 🍷

Grapes used to make: Zinfandel, Petite Sirah

Regions grown in: California, Croatia, South Africa, Australia

Body: Generally full bodied, but can also be medium, usually tannic, rich, big flavor

Flavors: Spice, smoke, berry, raspberry, blackberry, anise, black cherry, nuts, chocolate, pepper, jam, cinnamon, ginger

Notes: Zinfandel grapes produce a considerably high-alcohol wine, occasionally approaching the 15 percent alcohol mark. Raspberry and chocolate brings up a smoky essence, and spices can also work great with this peppery provision.

Chocolate Pairings

- 🍫 **Safe: Dark chocolate with chili pepper**
- 🍫 **Adventurous: Gluten-free chocolate chip oatmeal cookies***

6 White Wine and Chocolate Pairings

When I first started teaching chocolate and wine pairing classes, I rarely used white wines. As time passed, I started venturing into predictable whites such as Moscato d'Asti, Riesling, and even chardonnay. Now we're much bolder when pairing white wines with chocolate: we simply try everything to see what works. Personal research is definitely the best way to discover some of the mysteries of pairing.

White wines are often associated with white grapes, but the fact is that white wines occasionally include red or even black grapes. The skins are removed prior to fermentation to keep the wine white.

The sweetness of the wine depends on the length of time it's fermented, as well as how long the grapes are left on the vine. Wines start out fairly sweet, and as they're allowed to age, the grape's natural sugars are converted into alcohol. Longer processing equates to less sugar, more alcohol, and a drier wine.

More than 90 percent of the world's white wines come from three grapes: Riesling, sauvignon blanc, and chardonnay. A late harvest Riesling, which is a little sweeter, can be one of the best pairings for chocolate or a chocolate-based dessert. It all depends on your palate, of course. Chardonnay may be more difficult to pair because it's dry, but if you love Chardonnay and chocolate as well, chances are quite good that you'll be happy enjoying them together.

Other white grapes include chenin blanc, Viognier, Semillon, pinot grigio, pinot blanc, Albarino, and gewürztraminer, but this is far from the entire list. White wine enthusiasts will be thrilled to learn that there are more than fifty major white grapes varieties to explore.

As with the red wine discussion, you won't necessarily taste every flavor listed in the wine descriptions, but they're included to help you identify various possibilities. Refer to the "Wine Aroma Wheel" for more ideas. The more flavor names you have in front of you, the more flavors you'll taste. And just like the red wine section, all recipes with an asterisk (*) can be found in the back of this book.

CHABLIS

Grapes used to make: Chardonnay

Regions grown in: France/Chablis and Burgundy

Body: Medium to full bodied, long finish, dry

Flavors: Lemon, fig, flowers, steel, mineral, slate, green apple, earth

Notes: Chablis is produced from 100 percent white grapes, unlike many white wines, which contain a percentage of red grapes as well. Chablis normally pairs well with cream-based savory dishes, so consider adding a little cream to your chocolate when pairing as well. Because the wine is typically served chilled, let the chocolate dessert sit in your mouth for just a few seconds to begin to melt before you sip the wine.

Chocolate Pairings

> 🍷 **Safe: Chocolate Key Lime Pie with melted milk chocolate drizzled over the top**

Adventurous: Green apples dipped in melted milk chocolate and cinnamon

CHAMPAGNE

Grapes used to make: Chardonnay, pinot noir, pinot meunier

Regions grown in: France/Champagne (the only authentic Champagne), Italy

Body: Dry (brut), semidry (extra dry), semisweet (sec), sweet (demi-sec); white grapes make lighter Champagnes; red grapes make fuller Champagnes

Flavors: Grapefruit, lemon, citrus, apple, yeast, toast, mineral

Notes: Brut and extra dry are better served before and during dinner, while sec and demi-sec work better with chocolate and desserts. Finer Champagnes have smaller bubbles and more of them: look in the narrow part of the Champagne glass to see them best.

Chocolate Pairings

- Safe: Fresh strawberries dipped in white chocolate, a Champagne classic
- Adventurous: Potato chips dipped in milk or dark chocolate (believe it or not!)

CHARDONNAY

Grapes used to make: Chardonnay

Regions grown in: France/Burgundy, California, Australia, Chile, New Zealand, Long Island, Washington State

Body: Medium to full bodied, dry

Flavors: Green apple, citrus, lemon, pear, melon, toast, pineapple, vanilla, nuts, butter, wild mushrooms, peach, oak, herb, pear, kiwi, lime zest, jasmine, freesia, honeydew, mineral, earth

Notes: Chardonnay is often aged in oak barrels which gives it a rich, buttery flavor. But too much oak can make it tough to pair with chocolate, so you can also look for steel-aged Chardonnay for a little less oak. Get creative with fruit for your dessert options to help mellow the wine's natural acidity and bring up more of the fruit.

Chocolate Pairings

- **Safe: Vanilla cake with melted dark chocolate and a salted caramel ice cream on the side**
- **Adventurous: Apple cobbler topped with melted milk chocolate**

♟ CHENIN BLANC ♟

Grapes used to make: Chenin blanc

Regions grown in: California, France/Loire Valley, South Africa, Australia

Body: Crisp, dry wine with high acidity: ranges from very dry to sweet depending on the region where it's grown. Light to medium body, occasionally made as a dessert wine.

Flavors: Apple pie, pear, tart green apple, floral, honey, nuttiness, wax, damp straw, pepper, grapes, apricots, fruit flowers, mineral, melon, lime, nectarine, peach, quince, cloves, cream.

Notes: Chenin blanc offers up a bit of a challenge for chocolate pairing with its high acidity, so be prepared for a true pairing adventure! Note: later harvest chenin blanc's offer more chocolate-friendly flavors, like peach and pair.

Chocolate Pairings

- **Safe: Berry pie drizzled with melted milk chocolate and sprinkled with cinnamon**

- Adventurous: Vanilla pudding or tapioca sprinkled with milk chocolate chips

GEWÜRZTRAMINER

Grapes used to make: Gewürztraminer

Regions grown in: France/Alsace, California, Germany, Northern Italy, Washington State, Austria

Body: Medium bodied, lower acidity, low-alcohol; ranges from dry to sweet, depending on where the grapes are grown and the time they're harvested

Flavors: Allspice, clove, flowers, cinnamon, ginger, white pepper, rose water, lychee, citrus, honeysuckle, pink grapefruit, green apple, melon, apricot, peach, mint, licorice, roasted almond, fruit

Notes: Depending on how it's produced, this highly fruit-flavored wine is often quite sweet. Look for late-harvest Gerwürztraminer for added sweetness, which makes it better for a variety of chocolate pairings.

Chocolate Pairings

- Safe: Milk- or dark-chocolate-covered candied orange peel
- Adventurous: Ginger cookies dipped in pair jam and milk chocolate

MUSCAT/MOSCATO

Grapes used to make: Muscat

Regions grown in: France/Loire Valley, Greece, Italy/Piedmont, Australia, California, Chile

Body: Light, sweet, low in alcohol, often a bit bubbly. Wines from Alsace tend to be drier. Head to southern France for sweet dessert wines.

Flavors: Peach, apricot, orange, honey, spice, berry, tangerine, lemon, grape, musk, pear, white flowers; flavors vary depending on the region: Alsace and Samos have more tangerine; wines from Asti have more honey and floral notes.

Notes: The muscat grape is considered the oldest varietal of all grapes. This very sweet, low-alcohol dessert wine pairs wonderfully with orange fruits: oranges, apricots, peaches, mangos, papayas. Milk or dark chocolate, or both—why not?

Chocolate Pairings

- 🍫 **Conservative: Petite fours with milk/dark chocolate blend lightly swirled on top; sprinkle of cinnamon optional**
- 🍫 **Adventurous: Dark chocolate infused with organic lemon oil (available at www.TheChocolateTherapist.com, Wine Pairing Chocolates)**

🍷 PINOT BLANC 🍷

Grapes used to make: Pinot blanc

Regions grown in: Oregon, California, Italy/Alto Adige, France/Alsace

Body: Light to medium bodied, high acid, low sugar, clean, dry, crisp, long finish

Flavors: Melon, peach, nectar, honey, mineral, lime zest, nectarine, vanilla, wet stones, cider, chalk, lemon zest, walnut, green apple, spice

Notes: This clean, crisp wine makes a nice opening cocktail, guaranteed to wake up your guests and bring everyone into the moment. Like quite a few of the white wines, pairing with chocolate can be challenging, so get creative with your desserts and add chocolate as a possible side event.

Chocolate Pairings

- 🍫 **Safe: Shortbread cookies dipped in milk chocolate**

🍷 **Adventurous: Apple pie with melted 45% melted dark chocolate drizzled on top**

🍷 PINOT GRIGIO/GRIS 🍷

Grapes used to make: Pinot grigio or pinot gris

Regions grown in: France/Alsace, Italy, California, Oregon, New Zealand, Austria

Body: Dry with high acidity, although a late harvest from Alsace can be slightly sweet

Flavors: Lime, green apple, nectarine, orange, honey, clover, ginger, peach, mineral, earth

Notes: Like other white wines, pinot grigio's high acidity makes it challenging to pair with chocolate, but that doesn't mean it isn't possible. Milk chocolate can mellow it, and various fruits can bring out unique flavors.

Chocolate Pairings

🍷 **Safe: Raspberry tart with a small drizzle of melted 50% dark chocolate**
🍷 **Adventurous: Lemon biscotti dipped in melted milk chocolate**

🍷 RIESLING 🍷

Grapes used to make: Riesling

Regions grown in: Germany, Australia, France/Alsace, Washington State, New York, Austria, California/Sonoma, New Zealand, Italy, Canada, China, Italy

Body: Light bodied, crisp, sharp acidity, low alcohol: depending on the region, can be dry, semisweet, sweet, or sparkling

Flavors: Honey, flowers, apple, pear, peach, melon, mineral, petrol, kerosene, rubber, mango, guava, citrus, vanilla, apricot, orange, lime, slate, strawberry cream, lychee

Notes: Select a late-harvest Riesling when pairing with chocolate: you'll get a sweeter wine better suited to chocolate desserts.

Chocolate Pairings

- Safe: Peach cheesecake with melted chocolate drizzled on top
- Adventurous: Milk or dark chocolate covered orange peel

SAUVIGNON BLANC

Grapes used to make: Sauvignon Blanc, Semillon

Regions grown in: France, California, Australia, Chile, South Africa, Washington State, New Zealand

Body: Medium to full bodied, depending on the maker; medium to high acidity, crisp

Flavors: Grapefruit, green apple, gooseberry, fruit salad, hay, tangy, fresh herbs, lime, citrus, mineral, lemongrass, plum, straw, passion fruit, kiwi, pear, white peach, orange peel, cut grass

Notes: Over the years Sauvignon blanc has become one of my favorite wines to pair with chocolate, particularly milk chocolate, but it often works with dark chocolate and raspberry as well. They key is just to take a small bite of the dessert and add the wine after. Dryer wines come from Graves and Pessac-Leognan, while the sweeter options come from Sauternes and Barsac. The Marlborough region of New Zealand is also quite popular.

Chocolate Pairings

- **Conservative: Milk chocolate with key lime oil (available at www.TheChocolateTherapist.com, Pairing Chocolates)**
- **Adventurous: Dark chocolate bar infused with dried raspberries (try Chocolove).**

♟ SEMILLON ♟

Grapes used to make: Semillon, sauvignon blanc, Muscadelle, chardonnay

Regions grown in: France/Bordeaux, Australia, California, Washington State, Chile

Body: Full-bodied, varying acidic depending on the region

Flavors: Lime, lemon, apple, toast, cheese, peach, apricot, herb, honey, citrus, pineapple, vanilla

Notes: Semillon is more often blended with other grapes, rather than offered on its own. Dry wine enthusiasts will want to choose wines from the Sauternes region of Bordeaux. Those looking for something sweeter, which generally pairs better with chocolate, should look for wines from warmer climates like Australia, South Africa and Argentina.

Chocolate Pairings

- 🍫 **Safe: Dried peaches dipped in melted milk chocolate**
- 🍫 **Adventurous: Lemon cake with melted milk chocolate drizzled on top**

♟ SHERRY ♟

Grapes used to make: Palomino, Pedro Ximenez

Regions grown in: Germany, Spain, Italy, France

Body: Dry (manzanilla or fino), dry to medium (amontillado or oloroso), sweet (cream)

Flavors: Nuts, caramel, hazelnut, walnut, fig, molasses, dates, smoke, green apple

Notes: Sherry is a fortified wine, meaning neutral brandy has been added to the wine to raise the alcohol content. With sherry, the brandy is added after fermentation. In port, it's added during the process. Cream sherry pairs wonderfully with chocolate, but don't hesitate to venture into a variety of Sherry options.

Chocolate Pairings

- **Safe:** Peanut butter cookies dipped in milk chocolate
- **Adventurous:** Double Dark Chocolate Brownies* topped with caramel sauce and chopped almonds

♈ VOUVRAY ♈

Grapes used to make: Chenin blanc

Regions grown in: France

Body: Dry, semisweet or sweet

Flavors: Fruit, mineral, lemon, apple, pear, peach, flowers

Notes: Now is as good a time as any to pull out this much-loved cliché: "Like a box of chocolates, you just never know what you're going to get," unless, of course, you know your Vouvray. The wine varies greatly from region to region, like many of the white wines. Sweeter is better with chocolates, of course.

Chocolate Pairings

- **Safe:** Pumpkin pie with milk chocolate drizzle
- **Adventurous:** Chocolate peach cobbler* with chocolate sauce

♈ WHITE ZINFANDEL ♈

Grapes used to make: Zinfandel

Regions grown in: California

Body: Light, soft, low in alcohol, sweet, tangy

Flavors: Vanilla, cherry, orange, raspberry, lime, plum, strawberry, pineapple, pear

Notes: White zinfandel is made from red zinfandel grapes that have had the skins peeled off before fermentation. The resulting wine is very light, generally quite sweet, and often snubbed by true wine enthusiasts. Not all bad though, because that means more white zin for those who appreciate a relaxed, fresh wine that offers a collection of interesting chocolate pairings.

Adventurous Chocolate Pairings

- **Safe: Raspberry truffle brownies***
- **Adventurous: Pineapple upside down cake drizzled with milk chocolate**

Appendix A: Quick Reference Guide

Moscato	Pinot Noir	Zinfandel	Cabernet
Peach	Blueberry	Cinnamon	Cherry
Mango	Cashew	Pecan	Raspberry
Apricot	Milk chocolate	Nutmeg	Almond
Orange	Blackberry	Chili pepper	Blackberry
Nectarine	Hemp seed	Strawberry	Mint

Wine Shopping Strategy

You can either pair the wine with the chocolate or the chocolate with the wine. I generally start with the chocolate and pair it with the wine because I like chocolate more than wine. For me, having the perfect chocolate outweighs the importance of having the perfect wine. Many people, however, prefer to choose the wine first and pair the chocolate with the wine. Whichever you prefer, stick with quality on both the wine and the chocolate to give your pairings a better chance for success.

Smaller specialty shops generally offer wines that the owners or buyers have tasted and hand-selected. For diversity, look for stores with a nice international selection that includes wines from Argentina, Chile, South Africa, New Zealand, and Australia.

If you already have your chocolate or dessert idea in mind, look for wines that list similar flavors to what you're serving. Many wines have entertaining and informative descriptions on the labels, but if not, the store owner comes in handy, as well as various websites and wine apps (list of popular apps on page 54). Phones have made fact finding so much easier!

Appendix B: Chocolate and Wine Pairing Basics: A Summary

1. Taste both the chocolate and the wine in the same order as if you were at an individual chocolate-tasting or wine-tasting event. Sample lighter wines and chocolates first and move to heavier flavors from there.

2. Cleanse the palate with salt-free crackers or pretzels and drink room-temperature water between pairings.

3. It's best to limit the pairings to six wines and chocolates in a single event. Any more than that and taste buds may become desensitized, losing their ability to differentiate flavors.

4. Typically, light wines work better with a lighter chocolate, while the heavier, more-robust wines are better with darker chocolates. A heavy wine can overpower the chocolate, and vice versa.

5. Fortified wines (such as port and sherry) pair exceptionally well with chocolate because they're sweet and bold, making it possible for pairing success with a wider variety of chocolates.

6. For easy success with ports, pair them by their colors: Ruby port pairs well with ruby-colored infusions like berries, cherries, and strawberries. Tawny port generally works quite well with tan-colored infusions such as nuts, caramel, spices, and toffees

7. Wines with similar attributes as the chocolate work well together. For example, a fruity wine will better serve a chocolate with fruit nuances. This is called synergy: the two ideally match each other in some way and enhance the flavors of both.

8. You can either taste the wine and chocolate at the same time or try them separately. If you find the pairing is too tart together, try the wine first, followed by the chocolate.

9. Bittersweet chocolates generally go best with stronger red wines, especially wines that have a slightly roasted and bitter flavor with their own chocolate notes.

10. Milk and white chocolates pair well with dessert wines such as Moscato, port, sweet white wines, and even some dry white wines.
11. Tannic wines work better with rich, heavy chocolates with extra cocoa butter or cream. The butter in the chocolate helps mellow the tannic element of the wine, although the chocolate can still make the wine bite. If that happens, try them separately.

Great Wine Websites

Bon Appétit magazine	www.epicurious.com
Cellar Tracker	www.cellartracker.com
Decanter magazine	www.decanter.com
Food & Wine magazine	www.FoodandWine.com
French Scout	www.frenchscout.com
Gourmet Sleuth	www.GourmetSleuth.com
Happy Hour Alert	www.HappyHourAlert.com
Matching Food & Wine	www.MathchingFoodandWine.com
Professional Friends of Wine	www.WinePros.org
Snooth	www.Snooth.com
Wine Club Central	www.WineClubCentral.com
Wine Enthusiast Magazine	www.WineMag.com
Wine Intro	www.WineIntro.com
Winemaking	www.WineMaking.com
Wine Spectator magazine	www.WineSpectator.com
Wine.com	www.Wine.com

Great Wine Apps

Delectable
Vivino
Wine Ring
Wine Searcher
Hello Vino
Banquet
Drizly
WineRatings+

Appendix C: How to Microwave Chocolate

Many of the suggested wine and chocolate pairings call for you to make your own concoctions of melted chocolate with nuts, berries, spices, and naturally-flavored oils. This section will have you creating your own extraordinary recipes in no time. In just one to three minutes, your chocolate creation will be ready to go.

Chocolate is a bit finicky. When melted improperly, your delightful creation can turn into a scorched, "seized" chocolate mass. Fortunately, once you learn the technique, it's almost fail proof.

The main caveats in microwaving chocolate are: do it slowly and use low heat. It also works best when done in a glass bowl (not ceramic or plastic). Make sure there's absolutely no water in the bowl, or your chocolate may seize into an ugly chunk.

1. Pour the chocolate pieces into the bowl, up to about half full.
2. Reduce the microwave heat by 50 percent.
3. Microwave for thirty seconds, remove the bowl, and stir the chocolate (not much has happened yet).
4. Reduce microwave heat by 50 percent again.
5. Microwave again for thirty seconds, remove, and stir.
6. Let the chocolate begin to melt on its own.
7. Reduce heat to 50 percent, microwave, and stir again.
8. Repeat as needed, always remembering to reduce the heat by 50 percent each time you put the bowl back into the microwave.

Remove the chocolate just before it is completely melted and stir the remaining chunks until they melt. Melted chocolate is best for dipping, mixing, and serving immediately. It won't naturally harden into the same form it was in before you started unless you've tempered it, that is, heated it and then cooled it to the exact temperature required to reset the original form. If you want to dip chocolates that you plan to serve later, you'll need to refrigerate them to harden them.

Tempering is done to get chocolate to re-form beautifully once you've dipped or made whatever you're going to create. It's best done with a tempering machine. I've tried doing it in the microwave and on the stove with a candy thermometer, and it works great if you have plenty of time. I'm not going to cover all the details of tempering chocolate as it's quite complicated, but in general, milk chocolate should be brought to 86 degrees before pouring, and dark chocolate is 90-91 degrees. More information on how to temper chocolate is available on the internet.

Appendix D: Recipes

Chocolate Kahlua Truffles (Kristin Renzema)

12 ounces semisweet dark organic chocolate chips
½ cup heavy cream (*not* half-and-half)
½ stick butter (do not use margarine)
1 tablespoon instant coffee granules
2 tablespoons Kahlua
¼ tsp of salt
Cocoa powder for dusting

Combine all ingredients except the cocoa powder in a small saucepan. Heat over low heat, stirring occasionally until very smooth. Chill the mixture in a covered container, in the refrigerator until it's firm (approximately one hour). Take heaping tablespoons of the mixture, form them into one-inch balls, and roll each ball in the cocoa powder. Store the truffles in the refrigerator or the freezer for up to one month.

Chocolate Key Lime Pie

This is a speed baker's no-bake version.
1 can (14 ounces) of sweetened condensed milk
Juice from 4 limes
Juice from 2 lemons
1½ cups heavy whipping cream (or use 16 ounces Cool Whip)
¼ cup baking cocoa powder
4 tablespoons pure cane sugar or agave nectar
1 prepared graham cracker crust

In a small bowl, mix the milk with the juice of the lemons and limes and set aside. In a medium-sized bowl, mix the heavy cream with a mixer until it forms stiff peaks. Stir in cocoa powder and sugar, then add the juice-milk mixture. Stir until just mixed. Pour into prepared crust, and let refrigerate for at least one hour before serving.

Chocolate Whipped Cream

½ cup heavy cream
1 tablespoon cocoa powder
1 tablespoon pure cane sugar
Grated dark chocolate (optional)

In a medium bowl, whip cream with a mixer until it forms stiff peaks. Add cocoa powder and sugar (adjust amounts to personal taste) and blend in. To really impress guests, sprinkle some grated dark chocolate on top of the whipped cream.

Dark Chocolate Cake with Chocolate-Apricot Glaze

This is a speed baker's version, using a box of chocolate cake mix.
1 box chocolate cake mix, any brand
¼ cup baking cocoa powder

While preparing the cake according to the package directions, add the baking cocoa powder to the batter. Bake the cake according to box instructions and set aside to cool.

Chocolate-Apricot Glaze

1 cup pure apricot preserves (no sugar added)
½ cup orange juice
1 tablespoon agave nectar or honey
½ cup dark chocolate chips or chopped dark chocolate bar

In a small saucepan, combine preserves, orange juice, and agave nectar or honey and then stir over medium heat until melted. Reduce to low heat and stir in chocolate chips. Simmer uncovered on low heat for fifteen minutes or until mixture is thick enough to stay on the back of a spoon when dipped into the mixture. Drizzle or brush the glaze over the cake.

Dark Chocolate Vanilla Drizzle

8 ounces dark chocolate chips
1 teaspoon pure vanilla (do not use vanillin, an artificial flavoring)

Put the chocolate chips in a glass bowl. Microwave them on low heat, thirty seconds at a time, stirring each time until the chocolate is melted. Add the vanilla and stir. Drizzle onto pie, or anything else!

Double Dark Chocolate Brownies

This is a speed baker's rendition, using a boxed brownie mix.

1 box brownie mix, any brand

¼ cup baking cocoa

1 cup dark chocolate chips or 1 three-ounce dark chocolate bar, chopped

Preheat the oven to the temperature specified in the brownie mix directions. Follow the directions on the brownie box for mixing the batter. Add the cocoa and chocolate chips or chopped chocolate bar to the batter and bake the brownies according to the directions on the box.

Pomegranate & Cinnamon Dark Chocolate Brownies

Use the Double Dark Chocolate Brownies recipe, but when making the brownie mix, substitute pomegranate juice for the water in the recipe and add one teaspoon of cinnamon to the batter.

Gluten-Free Chocolate-Chip Oatmeal Cookies

½ cup shortening

¼ cup butter

¾ cup brown sugar

2 teaspoons pure vanilla extract

3 eggs

3 cups oat flour (make your own by grinding old-fashioned oats in the blender)

¼ cup dark organic cocoa powder

1 teaspoon baking soda

1 teaspoon salt

3 cup regular oats (not quick cooking)

2 3.5-ounce dark organic chocolate bars, chopped

¾ cup pecans, chopped (optional)

Preheat the oven to 350°F. In a large bowl, combine the shortening, butter, brown sugar, and vanilla and stir until blended. Add eggs and blend well. (Note: I prefer to stir cookie mix by hand because the cookies come out thicker and chewier than if you use an electric mixer, but feel free to choose either method.) Add the flour, cocoa powder, salt, and baking soda and mix well. Stir in the oats and mix well. Add the chopped chocolate and pecans (if using) and stir to distribute them throughout the mixture. Drop tablespoonfuls of the batter onto a lightly greased cookie sheet and bake for nine to ten minutes.

Haute Chocolate

To make this recipe lighter, substitute vanilla almond milk or rice milk, but note that the mixture will not get as thick as when you use half-and-half or whole milk. Also, you may want to try this without a sweetener, as the half-and-half makes the chocolate much sweeter.

4 ounces 65 percent or higher dark chocolate chips or chopped chocolate bar
2½ cups half-and-half or whole milk
3 tablespoons cocoa powder
½ teaspoon pure vanilla extract
2 tablespoons maple syrup or other sweetener (optional)
¼ teaspoon ancho or cayenne chili powder (optional)
Whipped cream and chopped nuts (optional)

Pour the half-and-half into a medium saucepan and turn the heat to medium, stirring constantly. Once hot, turn the heat to low, whisk in the chocolate and cocoa powder, and allow to simmer until the liquid has thickened slightly (make sure it doesn't boil). Add the vanilla, maple syrup, and ancho (if using), stir, then pour the liquid into four small coffee or tea cups. Garnish each cup with whipped cream and chopped nuts, if you prefer, and serve.

Raspberry/Pomegranate Purée

1 pound frozen raspberries, thawed and drained
½ cup pomegranate juice
2 tablespoons pomegranate juice
½ cup agave nectar, honey or raw cane sugar
1 tablespoon cornstarch

Combine the raspberries, half a cup of the pomegranate juice, and your sweetener of choice in a medium saucepan and bring to a boil; then allow it to simmer for fifteen minutes. Dissolve the cornstarch in the remaining two tablespoons of pomegranate juice and add this to the simmering mixture, stirring constantly. Continue to simmer until the purée is thickened. Spoon the purée over brownies, chocolate cake, chocolate pie, or the dessert of your choice.

Raspberry Truffle Brownies (Kristin Renzema)

¾ cup (1½ sticks) salted butter

4 ounces dark organic unsweetened chocolate, chopped

3 large eggs

2 cups sugar

⅓ cup raspberry jam

3 tablespoons black raspberry liqueur

1 cup all-purpose flour

¼ teaspoon salt

1 cup dark chocolate chips

Powdered sugar (optional)

Preheat the oven to 350°F. Spray a nine-inch-diameter springform pan with nonstick cooking spray. Melt the butter and chocolate in a large saucepan over low heat, stirring constantly until smooth. Remove from heat and set aside. Whisk in the eggs, sugar, jam, and liqueur. Stir in the flour and salt, then the chocolate chips. Transfer the batter to the prepared pan.

Bake the batter until a toothpick inserted in the center comes out with moist crumbs attached, about forty-five minutes. Let it cool in the pan on a rack for about an hour. When it has cooled completely, run a small knife around the edges of the pan to loosen it, then cut it into twelve squares. Dust the brownies with powdered sugar, if you prefer.

Tart Apple/Blackberry Pie

3 pounds thinly sliced green apples

1 pound fresh or frozen (thawed and drained) blackberries

¼ cup lemon juice

¾ cup pure cane sugar or raw sugar

½ cup flour (or ¾ cup oat flour for less gluten)

1 teaspoon cinnamon

½ teaspoon powdered cloves

Butter (softened)

Frozen pastry crust for single-crust pie, thawed and ready for baking

Preheat the oven to 375°F. In a large bowl, combine the apples, blackberries, and lemon juice and stir to coat the fruit with the lemon juice. In a small bowl, blend the sugar, flour, cinnamon, and cloves. Add the dry mixture to the apples and blackberries and toss until the fruit is well coated. Lightly butter the bottom of the piecrust. Pour the mixture into the piecrust and cover with foil. Bake the pie for thirty minutes. Remove the foil and bake for another thirty minutes, or until the apples are slightly soft (test lightly with a fork).

Dark Chocolate Truffles (Flavor variations below)

8 ounces whipping cream
½ cup (1 stick butter)
16 ounces 60 percent or higher dark chocolate, melted
Flavoring oils (see below)
Pure cocoa powder or cocoa powder and powdered sugar mixture

In a medium saucepan, heat the whipping cream over medium heat until it's boiling, stirring constantly. Remove from the heat, add the butter, and continue stirring until it's melted. Slowly add the butter and cream mixture to the melted chocolate. Add the various oils listed below, depending on the recipe.

Allow the truffle mixture to sit uncovered until it reaches room temperature, stirring occasionally. To speed up the process, the mixture can be put in the refrigerator until it reaches a consistency that can be rolled. Roll spoonfuls into half-inch balls, then roll each ball in pure cocoa powder, a cocoa powder and powdered sugar mixture, or various spices. The truffles can also be dipped in melted chocolate and refrigerated.

Add more flavors, if desired—the following recommendations are starting points. Note that if you have extra-strong flavoring oils, you may need less than these listed amounts. Start with small amounts and add a little at a time to flavor the truffles. The flavors listed here are oils, not flavorings or extracts. Oils are much stronger and are designed to flavor chocolates, so make sure you're using oils and not water-based extracts. You may purchase organic chocolate flavoring oils at www.NaturesFlavors.com.

Chili Pepper Truffles: ½ tablespoon chili oil

Coffee Ganache Truffles: ½ tablespoon coffee oil

Dark Chocolate Cherry Truffles: ½ tablespoon cherry oil

Raspberry Dark Chocolate Truffles: ½ tablespoon raspberry oil

Cinnamon Truffles: ½ teaspoon of cinnamon

References

Benjamin, Barbara Bloch. *The Little Black Book of Chocolate*. New York: Peter Pauper Press, 2003.

Coe, Sophie D., and Michael D. Coe. *The True History of Chocolate*. New York: Thames and Hudson, 1996.

Didio, Ton, and Amy Zovarto. *Renaissance Guide to Wine and Food Pairing*. Indianapolis, IN: Alpha Books, 2003.

Food and Wine Pairing.www.foodandwinepairing.org/food_pairing_board.html.

Jefford, Andrew. *Choosing Wine*. New York: Ryland Peter & Small, 2003.

Murdock, Linda. A Busy Cook's Guide to Spices: How to Introduce New Flavors to Everyday Meals. Denver, CO: Bellweather Book, 2007.

Murray, Michael T. *The Encyclopedia of Healing Foods*. New York: Atria Books, 2005.

The Pantry. Chocolate and Cocoa. Baking 911. Chocolate Basics. www.baking922.com/chocolate/basics.htm.

Nygard, Julie. *The Chocolate Therapist: A User's Guide to the Extraordinary Health Benefits of Chocolate*. Nashville, TN, Turner Publishing, 2018.

Raffaldini. www.raffaldini.com/grapes.shtml.

Red Wine Academy. www.redwineacademy.com/types-of-redwine-grapes.html.

Ristoraunte Amarone. www.loscabosguide.com/amarone/index.html.

Wine Folly. www.WineFolly.com

About the Author

Julie has embraced a passion for health and nutrition her entire life. A longtime competitor in sports, she was always interested in nutrition-for-performance. She studied nutrition and science in college and earned her degree in psychology from the University of Colorado in Denver.

Julie worked for Spyder Active Sports for twelve years before leaving to start her own company, then sold it five successful years later to follow her dream of becoming an author. Finally putting her passions together, she set out to prove that when you combine the mind, the body and chocolate, something extraordinary happens. A love for chocolate and a lifelong devotion to nutrition inspired Julie to write her first book about chocolate: *The Chocolate Therapist: A User's Guide to the Extraordinary Health Benefits of Chocolate*.

Julie speaks regularly to groups of all kinds including corporations, women's groups, men's groups, luncheons, non-profits, for educational programs and more. She's developed her own line of all-natural chocolate, teaches chocolate and wine pairing classes and has traveled internationally as a guest lecturer on cruise ships educating people about chocolate.

Dare to Pair was originally presented in *The Chocolate Therapist* under the "Chocolate and Wine Pairing" chapter, but the popularity of chocolate and wine pairing private parties as well as the classes at Julie's shop inspired her to release a completely updated and larger version of the chapter as its own book. *Dare to Pair* includes all of her most up to date discoveries in chocolate and wine along with a significant amount of material that has not been printed previously.

To book a speaking engagement or private event, contact Julie at Julie@TheChocolateTherapist.com.   Other books by this author:

THE CHOCOLATE THERAPIST:
A USER'S GUIDE TO THE EXTRAORDINARY HEALTH BENEFITS OF CHOCOLATE

All the health benefits of chocolate condensed into a one-stop resource for chocolate lovers worldwide. This book is easy to read, entertaining and educational--a great gift for every occasion.

Purchase: www.thechocolatetherapist.com
www.amazon.com (also available on kindle)

THE LAST DAMN DIET:
A STEP BY STEP GUIDE TO END YOUR WAR WITH FOOD FOREVER

After studying nutrition and how foods affect the body for more than 25 years, Julie has combined what she calls the "best of the best" secrets she's learned. This is a lifestyle program that you gradually adopt over time. You design it with *your* food, *your* schedule and *your* activities, custom tailored by you so you'll love it and stay on it forever.

Purchase: www.thechocolatetherapist.com

CHOCOLATE SOIREE:
HOW TO THROW THE ULTIMATE CHOCOLATE PARTY

Everything you need to know to host your own amazing chocolate party, including a 4-week planning guide, dozens of resources and references, and free printable materials that can be used at any party.

Purchase: www.thechocolatetherapist.com

A percentage of every sale on www.TheChocolateTherapist.com is donated to worldwide charity programs.

Made in the USA
San Bernardino, CA
13 July 2020